STEM CAREERS

CLIMATE SCIENTIST

by R.J. Bailey

pogo

Ideas for Parents and Teachers

Pogo Books let children practice reading informational text while introducing them to nonfiction features such as headings, labels, sidebars, maps, and diagrams, as well as a table of contents, glossary, and index.

Carefully leveled text with a strong photo match offers early fluent readers the support they need to succeed.

Before Reading

- "Walk" through the book and point out the various nonfiction features. Ask the student what purpose each feature serves.
- Look at the glossary together. Read and discuss the words.

Read the Book

- Have the child read the book independently.
- Invite him or her to list questions that arise from reading.

After Reading

- Discuss the child's questions. Talk about how he or she might find answers to those questions.
- Prompt the child to think more. Ask: Do you know anyone who works as a climate scientist? What projects has he or she been involved in? Do you have any interest in this kind of work?

Pogo Books are published by Jump!
5357 Penn Avenue South
Minneapolis, MN 55419
www.jumplibrary.com

Library of Congress Cataloging-in-Publication Data

Names: Bailey, R.J., author.
Title: Climate scientist / by R.J. Bailey.
Description: Minneapolis, MN: Jump!, Inc., [2017]
Series: STEM careers | Audience: Ages 7–10.
Includes bibliographical references and index.
Identifiers: LCCN 2017012833 (print)
LCCN 2017013826 (ebook)
ISBN 9781624965937 (ebook)
ISBN 9781620317167 (hardcover: alk. paper)
Subjects: LCSH: Climatology–Vocational guidance–Juvenile literature. | Climatologists–Juvenile literature.
Classification: LCC QC981.3 (ebook)
LCC QC981.3.B35 2017 (print) | DDC 551.6023–dc23
LC record available at https://lccn.loc.gov/2017012833

Editor: Jenny Fretland VanVoorst
Book Designer: Michelle Sonnek
Photo Researcher: Michelle Sonnek

Photo Credits: Adobe Stock: Alexander, 4. age fotostock: Dennis MacDonald, 14-15; Mint Images, 19. Getty: Paul Nicklen, 6-7, 11; QAI Publishing, 10; Erik Simonsen, 12-13. iStock: byllwill, 5. Shutterstock: Christoforos Acramidis, cover; olkapooh, cover; Photo Melon, cover; Pe3k, 1; Samuel Borges Photography, 1; Pete Pahham, 3; You Touch Pix of EuToch, 3; Pavel_D, 8-9; Cartarium, 10; Valeriy Lebedev, 10; Rocketclips, Inc., 14-15; ESB Professional 16-17; Toey Toey, 18; wavebreakmedia, 20-21; Benny Pieritz, 23.

Printed in the United States of America at Corporate Graphics in North Mankato, Minnesota.

ALPAC ELEMENTARY SCHOOL
310 MILWAUKEE BLVD. N.
PACIFIC, WA 98047

TABLE OF CONTENTS

CHAPTER 1

GETTING WARMER

Melting **glaciers**. Stranded polar bears. Fires. Droughts. Floods. Why is there so much bad news about the **environment**? It's because our planet's **climate** is changing. Earth and its oceans are getting warmer.

Unless we slow it down, this **climate change** will make life harder. In some places, there will be less food and water. Many animals will die.

Climate scientists are soldiers in this fight. They look for ways to reduce the effects of climate change. They look at ice. It can tell them a lot about climate history. They study weather patterns over time. Studying these trends can prepare us for changes ahead.

The climate has been changing for millions of years. But recent changes have been more dramatic than in the past. Most scientists believe **fossil fuels** are responsible. These fuels form gases when they burn. The gases build up. They trap heat energy from the sun. This produces a **greenhouse effect**.

TAKE A LOOK!

What is the greenhouse effect? Sunlight hits the planet. Some light reflects back into space. But gases have built up. They trap the light as heat. Earth gets warmer.

■ = sunlight
■ = gases

CHAPTER 2

WHAT DO THEY DO?

We know what is happening because of the work of climate scientists. But how do they learn what they know?

They spend time outside gathering **data**. They launch **weather balloons**. These balloons carry scientific instruments. They might measure temperature or wind speed. They might measure **humidity** or **air pressure**.

Climate scientists also get data from **satellites**. Satellites take pictures of the planet. The pictures show how weather changes over time.

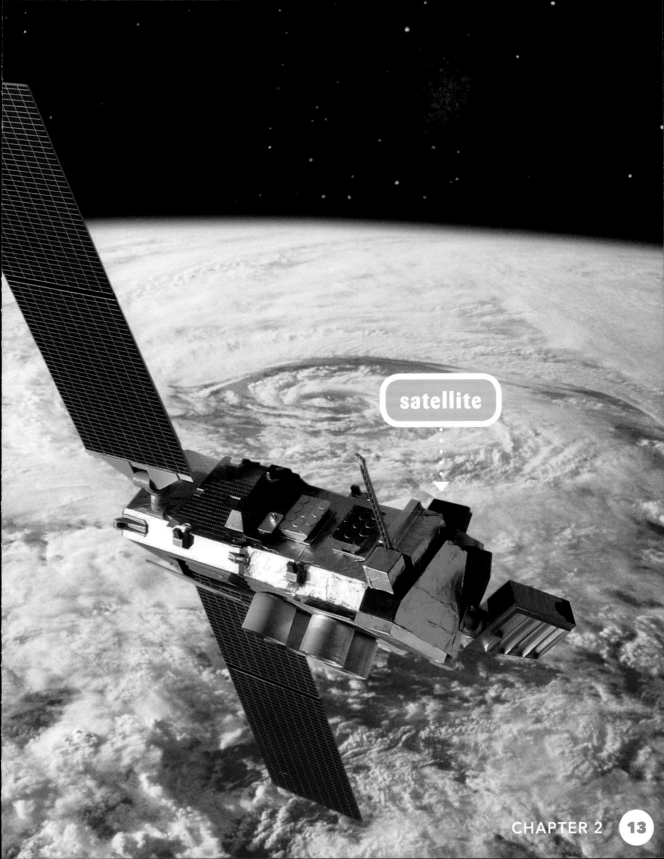

satellite

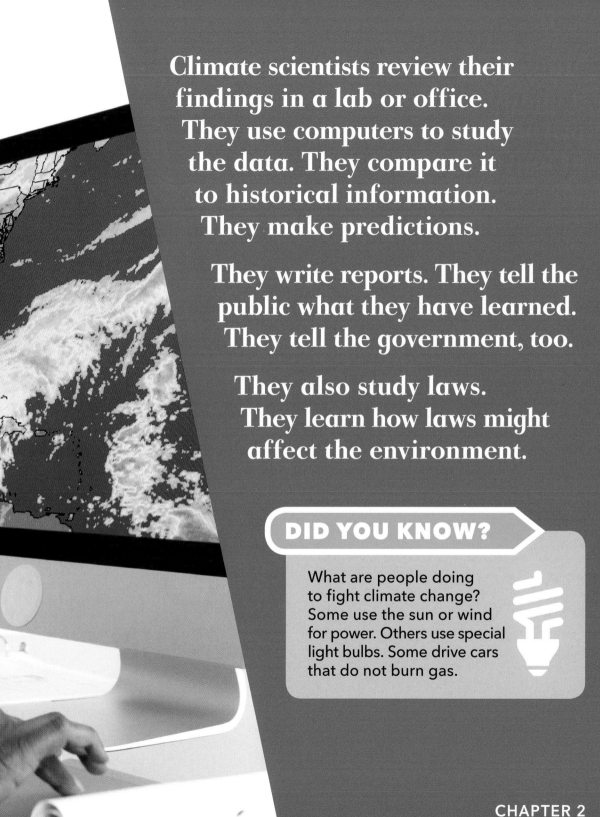

Climate scientists review their findings in a lab or office. They use computers to study the data. They compare it to historical information. They make predictions.

They write reports. They tell the public what they have learned. They tell the government, too.

They also study laws. They learn how laws might affect the environment.

DID YOU KNOW?

What are people doing to fight climate change? Some use the sun or wind for power. Others use special light bulbs. Some drive cars that do not burn gas.

Many climate scientists work for nonprofit groups. Others work for private companies. Some teach at universities.

CHAPTER 3

BECOMING A CLIMATE SCIENTIST

Do you care about the environment? Do you like finding answers to problems? Become a climate scientist!

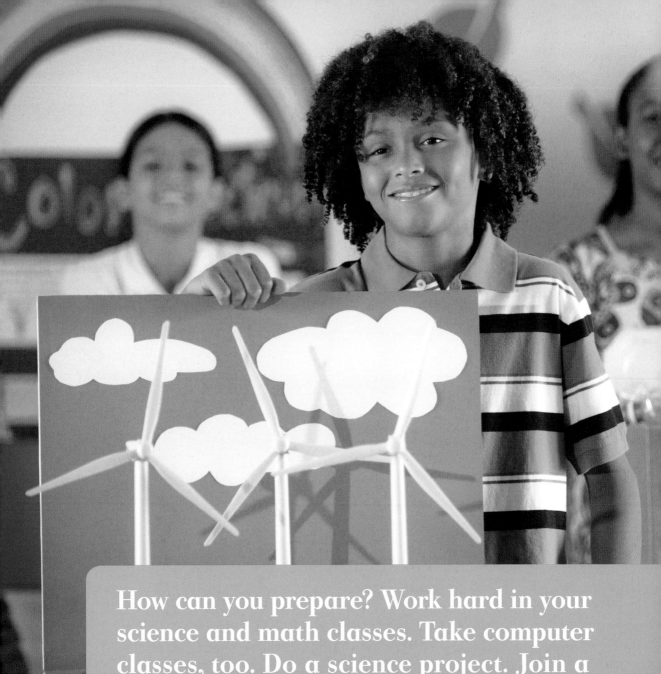

How can you prepare? Work hard in your science and math classes. Take computer classes, too. Do a science project. Join a science club. Get ready to take advanced classes in high school. Later you will need a college degree.

As a climate scientist, you can shape the future. How? You can show people how to reduce greenhouse gases. You can find ways to address problems like lack of food or water. You can make a difference!

DID YOU KNOW?

To work in this field, you need STEM skills. What does STEM stand for? Science. Technology. Engineering. Math. STEM careers are in demand. They pay well, too.

ACTIVITIES & TOOLS

CREATE THE GREENHOUSE EFFECT

A greenhouse takes in light and some heat energy from the sun. Heat builds up inside. To see this in action, make your own "greenhouse."

You Will Need:

- two glass jars that are the same size
- 4 cups of cold water
- 10 ice cubes
- clear plastic bag
- thermometer

❶ Fill each jar with 2 cups of cold water.

❷ Add five ice cubes to each jar.

❸ Cover one jar in the clear plastic bag. Seal it. This is your greenhouse.

❹ Put both jars in the sun for one hour.

❺ Record the temperature of the water in the uncovered jar.

❻ Record the temperature of the water in the "greenhouse" jar.

❼ Which jar has the warmer water? Did you expect it to? Why?

GLOSSARY

air pressure: The pressure exerted by the weight of air surrounding Earth.

climate: The common weather conditions of a particular area over a period of time.

climate change: A change in global or regional climate patterns, especially those within the past 50 years that are linked to the burning of fossil fuels.

data: Facts about something.

environment: The surroundings or conditions in which a person, animal, or plant lives.

fossil fuels: Fuels such as oil, coal, and natural gas that come from the dead plants and animals that have been trapped in the earth for millions of years.

glaciers: Large bodies of ice that move slowly on the land's surface and shape it as they move.

greenhouse effect: The warming that Earth experiences when greenhouse gases trap the sun's energy.

humidity: The amount of moisture in the air.

satellites: Machines that are sent into space to circle Earth, the moon, the sun, or another planet.

weather balloons: Large, helium-filled balloons that carry scientific instruments and are released into the sky to gather data on the weather.

INDEX

TO LEARN MORE

Learning more is as easy as 1, 2, 3.

1) Go to www.factsurfer.com
2) Enter "climatescientist" into the search box.
3) Click the "Surf" button to see a list of websites.

With factsurfer, finding more information is just a click away.